THE BUTCHER: NOLAN

THE BUTCHER: NOLAN

CHELSEA YASMINE WADE

Published by Spines Publishing Platform
ISBN: 979-8-89383-620-2

CHAPTER

ONE

For as long as I can remember, I was always destined to own my own meat shop. My father and grandfather both had their own shop, and it only seems fitting that I continue the family traditions. I now have a small shop here in a quiet and remote town. Perfect for my unique hobby. But we'll get to that later. I don't want to scare anyone just yet. First, let me explain my background, where I come from and why I do what I do.

People often see people like me as monsters, a devil, but honestly that's okay. It's okay because people in general are real monsters- rude, selfish and the list goes on. There are some good people, but we'll discuss that later. Oh, by the way, nice to meet you! My name is Nolan Prescott.

Screams...

"Come on now, Shane. Stop that! Why are you screaming? I'm not here to hurt you. I just want to talk."

He hoped this conversation would go one or two ways: Shane walks away as if nothing happened, or their friendship would end here and now.

"How could you do something like this Nolan? We've been friends our whole lives! What made you this way? Why were you hiding this from me?"

It was the way he said it, trying to wrap his head around what he had discovered about his oldest friend.

"I butcher people and feed them to others. Who are you to judge?"

"Like fucking Hannibal Lecter? You are insane!"

With a light chuckle, Nolan answered, "Well that's one way to put it, but no. I do what I do because I am tired of people who don't know what hard work is. To build from the bottom. People who look at you and me like we are less than because everything was handed to them. They are true scum."

As Nolan kept going on and on about his philosophy, Shane was trying to escape his ties.

"Stop trying to free yourself Shane. It's not going to work."

"Then you untie me." Shane said through gritted teeth.

Nolan wanted to untie Shane but not until they talked. Not until he understood why. Pacing back and forth, thinking about what to say to his oldest friend Nolan realized there really wasn't a good reason why he did what he did. Nolan grew up in a good but dysfunctional family. His father and grandfather spent a lot of time away from home. When asked what they were doing out so late they would just say they had things to take care of at the butcher shop. When Nolan was of age they shared their late-night adventures with him.

"This is how we start the hunt son," Nolan's father said with a smile. "And always remember son, the hunt never ends, it's only the beginning."

"Will you be quiet Here they come." Nolan's grandfather with a deep harsh raspy voice said as he nodded his head toward the man and women running down the street. As they turned down the dark alley the women stumbled and fell.

Nolan watched in awe as his father and grandfather moved with predatory grace. The thrill in their eyes was unmistakable. A shared family secret passed down through generations. It was a moment of initiation, a baptism into their twisted legacy. As Nolan kept watching his eyes filled with fear as his father looked back to him all Nolan could say was, "What the actual Fuck."

Shane's voice broke through Nolan's trance.

"You're sick, you and your whole family. You think you're some kind of vigilante, but you all are just murderers."

Nolan paused, looking at his friend. "Maybe we are Shane but, in my eyes, we are purging the world of the true parasites."

"You don't have to do this," Shane pleaded, his voice trembling. "We can go to the police and explain everything. You could get help."

Nolan sighed shaking his head. "It's too late for that. I'm too deep into this. And honestly, I don't want to stop."

Shane's eyes darted around, looking for any possible way to escape. But Nolan saw the realization settle in.

"What happens now?"

"Now?" Nolan stepped closer, a dark smile playing on his lips. "Now you understand, you are either with me or against me."

"I'll never be with you," Shane spat.

"Pity, I really hoped you would see things my way." Nolan replied tightening his grip on the knife.

In the dim light of the basement, the weight of their shared history pressed down on both of them. Shane's eyes filled with a mix of betrayal and sorrow, met Nolan's steely gaze. They had been through so much together, but this was a rift that could never be mended.

"How could you hide this from me?"

Nolan's face hardened, the mask of indifference slipping into place.

"Some things are better left unsaid Shane. Some secrets are too dangerous to share."

Nolan stood over Shane. He couldn't help but think of the first day they met. And with that Nolan whispered, "I'm sorry Shane." The finality of his words echoed in the cold dark room. "But this is the way it has to be."

CHAPTER

THREE

"I'm Shane Caldwell. What's your name?"

"Nolan Prescott. Let's be friends!"

And just like that two boys both aged seven became inseparable. They ran off into the summer afternoon, to the beginning of a long and seemingly unbreakable friendship that neither of them could have known would end in such darkness.

Shane and Nolan grew up in the same small town. Their lives were intertwined from the very beginning. They attended the same school, shared the same hobbies and spent countless hours exploring the woods and fields that surrounded their homes. Their bond was forged in the fires of childhood adventures and teenage trials. Shane was the more outgoing of the two, always ready with a joke and a smile. He was well liked, a natural leader among their group of friends. His easy-going nature made him popular.

Nolan in contrast was quieter, more reserved. He was thoughtful and observant, often content to let Shane take the lead. Despite their differences or perhaps because of them, they balanced each other perfectly. Shane's exuberance brought out the best in Nolan. Nolan's steady presence grounded Shane. As they grew older, they faced the unusual trials of adolescent school pressures. First loves, family struggles but they always faced them together. They dreamed of the future making grand plans for their lives, certain that their friendship would last forever. It wasn't until graduation that Shane went to college and worked part time at his family's hardware store and Nolan started working full time at the family's butcher shop.

One fateful night on a run, Shane accidentally discovered the true nature of the Prescott family business. It wasn't until then that everything changed. His shock, his horror at finding out his best friend was involved in something so sinister. Led to the confrontation that now threatened to tear them apart. Nolan walked up behind Shane, as they watched through the windows in the basement. In silence, Shane secretly admired Nolan's father and grandfather's work, the skill and pride they took in their craft, not knowing there was a darker side to their business.

"Why didn't you tell me your family business was such an art?"

Nolan's eyes looked over at Shane, "Because it's not the kind of art you think."

The innocence of their childhood and friendship meant everything to him. He could not tell his friend the truth that lies behind the closed doors of his family's business. Nolan had been forced into a different kind of loyalty a loyalty to the family legacy of the Prescott's.

"What kind of art is it then? Come on Nolan, we tell each other everything. Aren't we brothers?"

Shane finally turned to face Nolan. They stared at each other for a long moment and when the silence between them was too much to bear Nolan leaned over to Shane and said, "Some secrets are too dangerous to be shared. Even among brothers."

As the years passed, Shane never missed a chance to ask Nolan about the Prescott family business. Nolan would simply brush off his questions until they finally stopped coming. Despite the unspoken tension and the shadow of secrecy looming over them, Shane came to accept that some things in Nolan's life were off limits, as it was the same for him. As they grew into adulthood each of them pursuing their own paths, but always finding their way back to each other Nolan became more deeply involved in the family business, as did Shane with the hardware store. One night after work Shane decided to visit Nolan at the butcher shop. It had been a while since they had had a proper conversation. As Shane arrived at the shop, he found Nolan in the back room meticulously cleaning his knives.

"Hey Nolan," Shane greeted trying to sound casual. "Thought I'd drop by and see how you're doing. It's been a while."

Nolan looked up, his expression softening slightly. "Hey Shane, just the usual grind. What's up?"

Shane hesitated on his next words. Looking around the dimly lit room, he noticed something odd. No, it can't be, he thought to himself. Then the words came spilling out.

"Hey Nolan, is that a finger?"

Nolan signed, setting down his knives. He couldn't talk his way out of this one with Shane. All he knew was that things were different now. He has responsibilities and a legacy to uphold.

"Yes, that's a finger Shane."

Shane with widen eyes looked to Nolan understanding the secret he couldn't tell. Nolan, sensing the realization in

Shane's eyes stepped forward, with a hard darkened expression on his face.

"Are you killing people Nolan?" There was a long pause. "Is this the secret you couldn't...no, you wouldn't tell me?"

"I couldn't tell you! Family and loyalty! Yes, there were countless times I wanted to tell you, but I couldn't. Now that you know Shane, I can't let you leave."

In what seemed like a panic Shane started for the door, but Nolan got to him and hit him over the head, knocking him out. Nolan tied him up in a chair and waited for him to wake up.

CHAPTER
FOUR

Nolan stood over Shane's body, a strange mix of sadness and satisfaction washing over him. He knew this was the end of one chapter and the beginning of another. Wiping the blades clean he whispered, "Welcome to the family business Shane."

As Nolan locked up the shop, he knew his secret was safe for now. But, deep down, he also knew that it was only a matter of time before someone came looking for Shane. The hunt, as his father and grandfather taught him, never truly ended. It was only the beginning. The next day Nolan opened the shop like any other day. The usual customers came in exchanging pleasantries, oblivious to the horrors that transpired the night before. Nolan's mind was elsewhere thinking about his next move. In the afternoon a stranger walked into the shop. Dressed in a long coat and hat, the person's face was partially obscured by shadows. Nolan's instincts kicked in; this wasn't a regular customer.

"Can I help you with something?" Nolan asked, trying to keep his tone neutral.

The stranger looked around the shop before speaking. "I'm looking for someone, a friend of mine, Shane Caldwell. Have you seen him?"

Nolan's heart skipped a beat, but he kept his composure. "Shane? No, I haven't seen him in a while. Is everything okay?"

The stranger stepped closer, his eyes narrowing. "Funny, because the last place he was seen was near your shop. You sure you haven't seen him?"

Nolan forced a smile. "I'm positive. If I do see him, I'll be sure to let him know you're looking for him."

The stranger held his gaze for a moment longer before nodding. "I'll be back," he said turning to leave.

As the door closed behind him Nolan's mind raced. He needed to be careful. The stranger was clearly on to something, and Nolan couldn't afford any mistakes. Later that night Nolan went to the basement of his shop, where he kept his "tools" and "supplies." He stood over Shane's body, now cold and lifeless thinking about his next move. He knew he couldn't keep Shane's body forever. His father's voice echoed in his mind. "Always clean up your mess Nolan. Leave no trace."

He got to work dismembering Shane's body with precision and efficiency. This wasn't his first time, and he knew it wouldn't be the last. As he worked he thought about the stranger and what he might know. He needed to find out who he was and how much he knew. The following day Nolan decided to take a walk around town, trying to see if he could gather any information. He visited the local diner, a hub of gossip and news. As he sipped his coffee, he overheard a conversation between two patrons.

"Did you hear about Shane? He's gone missing," one of them said.

"Yeah, and there is this private investigator in town

looking for him. Real serious guy. Said he wouldn't leave until he finds out what happened," The other replied.

Nolan's suspicions were confirmed. The stranger was an investigator, and he had to act fast. He needed to find a way to throw the investigator off his tail. That night, Nolan decided to visit Shane's house. He broke in searching for anything that could help him. As he rummaged through Shane's belongings, he found a notebook filled with entries about their friendship, Shane's suspicions about Nolan, and detailed notes on his activities.

"This is bad," Nolan muttered to himself. He knew he had to destroy the notebook before the investigator found it. As he was about to leave, he heard a noise outside. The investigator was there, standing at the front door. Nolan quickly hid in the shadows clutching the notebook. The investigator entered, flashlight in hand, searching the house. Nolan knew this was his chance. As the investigator moved to another room Nolan slipped out the back door and disappeared into the night.

The next morning the investigator visited Nolan's shop again.

"Good morning," Nolan greeted, trying to appear calm.

"I think you know more than you are letting on," the investigator said bluntly. "I found some interesting things at Shane's house. Care to explain?"

Nolan feigned ignorance. "I have no idea what you are talking about."

"I'll be watching you, Nolan. I know you are hiding something, and I will find out what it is."

As the investigator left Nolan knew the game was on. He needed to be smarter, more careful. The hunt was no longer just about his prey; it was about his survival.

"The hunt never truly ended, it's only the beginning."

FIVE

Days turned into weeks, and the investigator grew more persistent. Nolan continued his façade of normalcy, but the pressure was mounting. One evening, as he was closing up the shop, he found a note slipped under the door

"I know what you did. Meet me at the old barn tonight."

Nolan's heart pounded. Who could have left the notes? Was it a trap? He knew he had to go but he had to be prepared. As he arrived at the old barn, he saw a figure standing in the shadows. It was the investigator.

"I knew you would come," the investigator said.

Nolan took a step forward. "What do you want?"

"Justice for Shane," the investigator replied. "I have all the evidence I need to take you down." Nolan felt a surge of anger. "You think you can stop me? You have no idea what I am capable of."

"Oh, I think I do," smirked the investigator.

In a flash, the two men clashed, a violent struggle ensued. Nolan fought with the ferocity of a cornered animal, but the investigator was equally determined. In the end, Nolan stood over the investigator, bloodied but victorious.

"You should have stayed out of my business," Nolan said breathing heavily.

As he looked around the barn, Nolan knew he had to clean another mess. He couldn't leave any evidence behind. With the investigator's body disposed of, Nolan returned to his shop and placed the meat on display and went down to the basement. He was weary but resolved. He knew this wouldn't be the last time someone came looking for answers. But he was ready.

The hunt, as his father taught him. Never truly ended. It was only the beginning.

CHAPTER

SIX

Waking up, Shane couldn't shake the feeling that something was deeply wrong. Rubbing his head where Nolan had hit him, "Still tender." He whispered to himself.

"Feeling any better?" a familiar voice came from around the corner. Nolan? It was Nolan.

"What happened?" asked Shane.

"You came to see me a few nights ago. I told you I kill people and sell them as meat to others, and you passed out. By the way, that detective you were working with was looking for you."

There was a pause, and Shane's eyes widened with a sharp look. He turned to Nolan.

"Did you kill him?"

With a long sigh Nolan shortly stated, "Yup, he's today special at the shop."

Nolan couldn't cope with the emotions of killing his oldest friend. Seeing Shane's limp unconscious body pained him deeply. He couldn't imagine being without his best friend. As

Shane sat there in the chair Nolan's final conclusion led him to keep Shane in the shop until he woke. He figured he could work things out with him. He hoped for the best with a conversation with Shane.

Shane walked over to the table where Nolan already had a cup of coffee waiting for him.

"I have done this every day for the past few days," Nolan said.

"When you say a few days what do you really mean? You forget I know you best. A few days could mean "A few days" or it could mean "A few weeks." So, which is it?"

"Weeks, two to be exact. That's how long you have been out."

Nolan turned to face Shane with a smile. "I must have hit you pretty hard."

Shane's eyes widened as memories flooded back. He remembers coming to visit Nolan, which happened to be a while since he saw him. Walking in on the discovery of the human finger and being hit over the head...Then nothing.

"Oh, yeah that's right. The finger, were you keeping it as a snack? That's creepy."

"A snack, sure I like crusty old men's fingers." Nolan says.

Nolan gave him a puzzled look.

"You are not willing to take me to the police and get help? You pleaded so much for me to stop this madness?"

Shane throws a wicked smile at Nolan and replies, "We can still take you to get help, but we do not need to get the police involved. Besides I was hit over the head and was out for two weeks. Would they even believe me?"

Nolan gave him a look like yeah, you're right, no one would.

"Why?" Shane croaks, his voice barely a whisper. "Why didn't you kill me?"

Nolan chuckles, finding Shane's gaze. "You're my best friend Shane. I didn't want to lose you. Besides I know you want in, don't you? When we were kids, you seemed so interested."

Shane's heart pounded. He had been curious yes but that was before he knew it was human meat.

"What are you talking about?"

Nolan stands up pacing the room.

"I saw the look in your eyes when you found out that night you came to see me, and then before when we were kids. Not just fear. There was something else. Curiosity, excitement even. Don't deny it. Your thoughts before where what if they were cutting up a person?"

Shane swallows hard. "I...I don't know what you think you saw, or what you are talking about. But"-

Nolan interrupts, his tone turning serious. "I saw a partner that night, someone who could help me take over the family business, and now you have no choice. You're in this Shane. I want you in this. Whether you like it or not."

CHAPTER
SEVEN

I'm in this weather I like it or not huh? I do not understand, how did he know I was thinking that that night? I fell in love with the way his family was so passionate about their blade work. Each cut, each slice looked so beautiful. Not realizing that the reason they looked so meticulous was because they were cutting up people, actual people! Should I be so surprised? I mean I have secrets too. Secrets I never told Nolan. If things were different and Nolan was trying to figure out why I was MIA for weeks or even months at a time and ended up finding out my secret, would he react the same as me? No, it wouldn't be the same. If Nolan found out my secret, he would be more excited. He said he saw a partner in me. Maybe that's what I need for my hobby. To be excited that I found out about this secret. Understanding the late nights and long trips, but I can't let him know I'm excited. Oh, I am so very excited, but for now let's go back.

After leaving the woods after hanging out with Nolan all day, Shane sensed there was something a little off about Nolan this time. Since graduating high school, Shane has been attending classes at the local college part time and working at the family hardware store. While Nolan was now working full time with his father and grandfather in the butcher shop. For 2 weeks at a time, sometimes even for a month Nolan, his dad and grandfather travel out of town, and when they return Nolan seems to be more closed off and quiet than usual. Driven by a growing sense of unease and the need to protect his friend, or at least find out what's going on. Shane starts to feel a little stress and the need to release some tension. So, after dinner with his family, he decided to go for a run.

"Is everything okay young man?"

"Yes, I was just trying to catch my breath," Shane said in a breathy chuckle.

"Oh okay, are you sure? I can help you back to your car or over to that diner. It's no problem."

She seemed really nice. Looking up at her he thought she might be there visiting because he did not recognize her face. As he kept looking at her he nodded toward the bench. It was shaded by some trees off to the side of the trail he was running on. Nobody would notice if anyone was sitting there unless they were close enough to see.

"Thank you for your help. You are nothing but kind. I wish more people were like you."

"Thank you," she said as she helped Shane sit on the bench.

"Are you from here? I don't think I ever saw you around here seeing how this is a small town and all."

"No, I'm just making a stop. My car broke down a mile up the road and I just wanted to see if I could get any help and then I saw you." She smiled.

That beautiful smile and light brown eyes, Shane thought.

"Well since you helped me out, I know a thing or two about cars. Let me take a look. That is if you want me to."

"Oh yes please! Are you okay to walk?" She asked.

There goes that smile. Shane might have done her in right there, but he wanted to take his time with this one. She's so beautiful.

After resting for a while they headed to her car. When they were out of view of any other bystanders that's when it happened. Shane blacked out. When he woke up, he found himself in his hardware store's basement with the woman who just helped him. Tied to a chair Shane was watching her, as her eyes flutter open and suddenly go wide with fear. He was standing there laughing, waiting to hear her scream. Shane loved it when they screamed. It makes this much more exciting. No one could hear them anyway. They were in a hidden room that led down to a secret door to where his basement was. Nobody would know it was there unless they were looking for it. To the naked eye it just looks like another storage closet. Soundproof anyone can scream all day and no one would even hear them.

CHAPTER

EIGHT

I t was a typical morning at Prescott's butcher shop. The sound of knives being sharpened. The rhythmic chopping of meat and the low hum of the refrigeration units created a symphony of everyday life in the shop. Nolan worked with practice precision his mind wondering about the recent events and the new dynamic with Shane. Shane, now fully integrated into the business, was now manning the counter and greeting customers with a newfound ease. The bell above the door chimed, signalling the arrival of another customer. Shane looked up, ready to deliver his rehearsed smile and greeting, but hesitated when he saw the man who entered. The man was tall with a weathered face and a piercing gaze. He wore a dark coat, which he didn't remove despite the warmth of the shop. He approached the counter slowly, his eyes scanning the room with an intensity that made Shane uneasy.

"Morning," the man said, his voice calm but authoritative. "I'm looking for some information. Maybe you can help."

Shane's heart raced, but he maintained his composure. "Sure, what can I do for you?"

The man pulled out a photograph and placed it on the counter.

"Have you seen this man? His name is Detective Daniels. He's been missing for a few weeks. He was last seen in this town."

Shane glanced at the photo, his stomach knotting. He shook his head, "Can't say that I have. You should try the police station. They might know something."

The man's eyes narrowed slightly. But he nodded. "I'll do that thanks."

He took back the photo and turned to leave but not before casting a lingering look around the shop. Later that day Nolan noticed Shane's unease and approached him as they took a break in the back room. The tension in the shop was palpable after the stranger left.

"What's wrong?" Nolan asked, handing Shane a cup of coffee. Shane took a sip, his hands trembling slightly.

"Some guy was asking about the missing detective. He showed me a photo of a man. I recognized him, but it felt off."

Nolan's expression darkened. "We need to be careful. If someone's looking for that detective it means we might have more eyes on us."

With Shane's concerned look, he says, "More eyes on us? What does that mean Nolan?"

"Nothing right now. We just need to be careful. Let's finish the day and talk about this later. Do you think you can do that?" Nolan asked with a slight smile.

"Yes, let's get back to it."

CHAPTER

NINE

Detective Alex Morgan walked out of the butcher shop, his mind already working through the implications of the brief conversation. He had noticed Shane's nervousness and the subtle tension in the air. It wasn't much, but it was enough. He drove to the local police station and introduced himself to the chief.

"Detective Morgan, FBI I'm looking into the disappearance of my partner Detective Daniels. He was working on a case here before he went missing."

The chief a burly man with a gruff demeanor leaned back in his chair. "Daniels, yes, I remember him being here a few weeks ago. He was also looking for someone as well."

Morgan nodded, "I see, I'd like to see his files and notes he left behind. May they carry some insight into where he might be."

"I do not have any files. He came in just as you are now asking for someone who isn't even missing. After that no one saw him again."

Morgan looked puzzled. "Do you remember the person he

was looking for? They might be able to help point me in the right direction."

The chief sat up looking sharp in the detectives' eyes. "Yes, he was looking for Shane Caldwell. He works at the Prescott Butcher shop."

Morgan's eyes narrowed. He just came from the shop. It was a lead and he must follow through thoroughly.

TEN

As work ended for the day, Shane was still feeling unease about the encounter with the Detective coming into question him about the man he hired to help look into his friend. Nolan noticed, and once he put up the closed sign, he motioned for Shane to follow him to the back room.

"Tell me everything. What you are thinking, how you feel, everything."

Shane sat in a chair in the corner with his head in his hands. He took a deep breath and let it out. "I don't know if I can do this. The detective is going to find out you're the one who killed his partner. And I was the one who brought him here to look into you. What are we going to do Nolan?"

Nolan's expression hardened as he paced the small room, the flickering light casting shadows on the wall.

"We stick to the plan," he said firmly. "We knew this could get complicated. The important thing is not to panic. The detective doesn't have concrete evidence yet."

"But we don't know what he already knows."

Shane interjected, his voice trembling. "What if he comes

back with more questions? What if he finds out about the barn?"

Nolan stopped pacing and turned to Shane, his eyes cold and calculated. "Then we make sure he doesn't find anything. We need to go back tonight. Make sure it looks like nobody has still never been there."

Shane nodded slowly, his mind racing. "And what about the detective?"

Nolan's jaw tightened. "We can deal with him if we need to but for now, we stay calm and cover our tracks. You understand?"

Shane swallowed hard and nodded. "Yeah, I understand."

Nolan clapped him on the shoulder "Good, now let's get to work we don't have much time."

The next morning, Shane arrived at the shop early, his nerves on edge. Nolan had stayed up most of the night orchestrating the moves of their plan. He hoped it would be enough to throw off any suspicions. Just as he was about to open the shop, Detective Morgan walked in, his face stern and serious.

"Good morning, Shane." Morgan said, his tone cold and direct. "We need to talk."

Shane felt his stomach churn. He threw a quick glance at Nolan.

"Of course, Detective. What's this about?"

Morgan pulled out the photo of Daniels again. "My partner was looking for you. He believed you were missing. Why is that? Assuming you lied to me yesterday about not knowing him. Why did he think you were missing?"

Shane's mind raced searching for the rehearsed excuse, but his mouth was dry. He took a deep breath, trying to maintain his composure.

"I...I didn't lie Detective. I just didn't recognize him at first."

Morgan's eyes narrowed his skepticism evident. "You didn't recognize him? That's odd, considering you two have a history."

Shane's heart pounded in his chest. "History? What are you talking about?"

Morgan leaned in, his voice low and menacing. "Don't play dumb with me Shane. Daniels was investigating a series of disappearances, and your name came up more than once. Now he's missing and you're acting like you don't know anything about it."

Shane's mind was a blur of panic and confusion. He tried to recall everything Nolan had told him, but it was slipping away.

"I swear Detective I don't know what happened to Daniels. I haven't seen him in a few months."

Morgan's gaze was unwavering. "If you are lying to me Shane I will find out and when I do there will be consequences."

Just then Nolan walked into the shop from the back room having heard the conversation. His expression was calm and composed. "Is there a problem here Detective?" He asked, his tone polite but firm.

Morgan straightened up his eyes flickering between them both.

"Just making sure things are in order, Mr..." Morgan said with an out reaching hand.

"Prescott, Nolan Prescott. I own this butcher shop."

"Mr. Prescott," Morgan says shaking his hand. "Like I said just making sure things are in order. We don't want any misunderstandings now do we?" Morgan looked back at Shane.

Nolan smiled. There was no warmth in it. "Of course not.

We are happy to cooperate with your investigation, isn't that right Shane?"

Shane nodded, trying to muster a confident smile. "Yes of course."

Morgan held their gaze for a moment longer before nodding. "I'll be in touch." He said turning to leave.

As soon as he was out of earshot Shane turned to Nolan, his voice a whisper. "He knows something Nolan. What are we going to do?"

Nolan's smile faded, replaced by a steely determination. "We stick to the plan. We don't break you understand?"

Shane nodded, but the fear in his chest only grew. The detective was getting close, and he did not know how much longer he could keep up with this façade. The noose was tightening, and he could only hope that Nolan's resolve was enough to save them both.

TWELVE

The next few weeks were a blur of tension and close calls. Detective Morgan returned several times, questioning them and scrutinizing every detail. Nolan remained unflappable, always one step ahead, providing just enough information to keep Morgan at bay but never enough to incriminate them.

Finally, for what had seemed like an eternity Morgan stood in the shop one last time.

"It seems we've exhausted all leads." He said his frustration barely concealed. "For now, you're free to go about your business. But, know I will be watching you both."

Nolan nodded; his expression carefully neutral. "We understand Detective Morgan. Thank you for your diligence."

Morgan gave one last hard look before turning on his heels and walking out of the shop. Shane exhaled a breath he didn't realize he was holding.

"Is it really over?" Shane asked his voice shaky.

Nolan placed a reassuring hand on his shoulder. "For now,

yes, we've covered our tracks well. Just remember we need to be more careful from now on."

Days turned into weeks and weeks into months. The shop returned to its normal routine and the shadow of the investigation slowly faded. Shane and Nolan fell back into their familiar rhythm, their bond and friendship stronger than ever. Years passed and the memory of Detective Morgan became a distant echo. Shane had grown more confident, more assured under Nolan's tutelage. He knew that their way of life required constant vigilance, but he also knew he had to learn from the best. One evening as they were closing up the shop Nolan turned to Shane with a serious expression on his face.

"It's time," he simply said.

Shane knew what Nolan meant. This was the moment that would solidify his place alongside Nolan.

"I'm ready," Shane replied, his voice steady.

With the same smile his father had had when he and Nolan's grandfather finally shared the family secrets with him, Nolan recited, "The hunt Shane, never really ended, this is only the beginning."

They drove in silence to a remote location. The tension in the air was palpable. Nolan had chosen the target carefully just as his grandfather would. Someone that wouldn't be missed. Someone who has done wrong in the world. Someone who had everything handed to them. Someone who felt they were above the law and everyone else. As they parked the car and stepped into the shadows, Nolan handed Shane the knife, its blade gleaming in the moonlight.

"Remember, stay calm, be precise and show no hesitation," Nolan instructed.

Shane nodded, his grip tightening around the handle. He took a deep breath, focusing on the task ahead as they approached their target. He felt a strange mix of fear and exhilaration. This was the pinnacle of everything he had learned. In the quiet darkness, Shane moved with purpose. Nolan's presence behind him was a steadying force, a reminder that he was not alone. As he made the final approach, he felt a surge of adrenaline. With one swift, decisive motion, he plunged the knife into the target. The man's gasp was brief, his struggle quickly fading. Shane stood over him, his heart pounding in his ears. He had done it. He had crossed the line. Nolan stepped forward, placing a hand on Shane's shoulder.

"Well done," he said quietly. "You did well."

Shane looked at Nolan meeting his gaze. There was pride in his best friend's eyes. A silent acknowledgement of his transformation. As they left the scene, a new sense of purpose settled in Shane. He wasn't just a best friend, a childhood friend or a brother. He was a partner.

THIRTEEN

The shop opened as usual the next day, with a new meat special on display. Things have changed. Shane had his first kill and there was no turning back. Nolan would continue their carefully orchestrated lives, always one step ahead, always in control. They knew what they were given was fraught with danger, but they also knew they were prepared to face it together. Just like they faced everything together as kids. After cleaning the back room from chopping the meat Nolan entered the front of the shop meeting Shane.

"How are you holding up?" His tone was uncharacteristically gentle.

Shane took a breath, considering his question.

"I'm okay Nolan. Better than I thought I would be. It feels...right."

Nolan nodded, a hint of a smile on his lips. "Good that's important. It gets easier with time, but the first one is always the hardest."

Shane met Nolan's gaze. A steely determination in his eyes. A darkness inside him.

"I'm ready for the next one."

Nolan studied him for a moment, then nodded in approval.

"You're ready for the next one?" He affirmed. "We'll take it step by step just like we planned. You did well Shane."

Shane felt grim satisfaction. He was finally where he belonged, and he was ready for Whatever would come next.

"What do you mean you came to a dead end? That doesn't make sense Alex. You were my husband's partner's best friend even. You should have torn that town apart looking for him. I don't trust anyone but you to finger this out. Please, for me. I need to know what happened to him and make sure the one or ones responsible also meet their end for what they did to my husband."

She looks at me with sadness and anger. I failed her and Daniels. Alex's phone buzzed with a text alert. He opened opened it. His eyes widened. A video of two familiar faces killing a man.

"I knew it. I will bring justice to you and Daniels don't you worry about that."